DATE DUE

Great African Americans

Jesse Owens

olympic star

Revised Edition

Patricia and Fredrick McKissack

Series Consultant
Dr. Russell L. Adams, Chairman
Department of Afro-American Studies, Howard University

 Enslow Publishers, Inc.

40 Industrial Road	PO Box 38
Box 398	Aldershot
Berkeley Heights, NJ 07922	Hants GU12 6BP
USA	UK

http://www.enslow.com

921
Owe
id
200 13.95

To Our Friend, (Sir) Christopher Powell

Revised edition of *Jesse Owens: Olympic Star* © 1992

Library of Congress Cataloging-in-Publication Data

McKissack, Pat, 1944–
    Jesse Owens : Olympic star / Patricia and Fredrick McKissack.— Rev. ed.
      p. cm. — (Great African Americans)
    Includes index.
    Summary: Describes the life of the sharecroppers' son who became an
Olympic legend, and challenged Hitler's dream of Aryan superiority.
    ISBN 0-7660-1681-1
    1. Owens, Jesse, 1913–1980—Juvenile literature. 2. Track and field athletes—United States—
Biography—Juvenile literature. [1. Owens, Jesse, 1913–1980. 2. Track and field athletes.
3. Afro-Americans—Biography.] I. McKissack, Fredrick. II. Title.
    GV697.O9 M35 2001
    796.42'092—dc21   00-009424

Printed in the United States of America

10 9 8 7 6 5

To Our Readers: We have done our best to make sure all Internet addresses in this book were active and appropriate when we went to press. However, the author and the publisher have no control over and assume no liability for the material available on those Internet sites or on other Web sites they may link to. Any comments or suggestions can be sent by e-mail to comments@enslow.com or to the address on the back cover.

Every effort has been made to locate all copyright holders of material used in this book.
If any errors or omissions have occurred, corrections will be made in future editions of this book.

Illustration Credits: Associated Press, pp. 3, 10, 11, 12, 13, 15, 16, 17, 19, 21, 22, 24, 25, 26; Library of Congress, pp. 6, 7, 8; Courtesy of USHMM Photo Archives, p. 16.

Cover Credit: Associated Press

TABLE OF
CONTENTS

James CLeveLand (Jesse) Owens

September 12, 1913–March 31, 1980

CHAPTER 1

From J.C. to Jesse

Henry Owens was a poor farmer in Oakville, Alabama. His wife, Emma, washed and ironed other people's clothes for extra money. The Owens family worked very hard. But they were still poor.

Henry Owens and his family were sharecroppers. A big landowner let them grow cotton on a small piece of his land. They gave most of their cotton to the landowner to pay for the land. They sold the little bit that was left so they could buy food and

This is the way most sharecroppers lived in the early 1900s.

other things they needed. They could not save any money.

James Cleveland Owens was born in 1913. He was Henry and Emma's tenth child. They called him J.C. He was a sickly baby. His parents were afraid that he might not live.

6

J.C. was sick every winter. His lungs were weak. J.C.'s mother and father did not have money to pay a doctor. They took care of him the best way they could.

J.C.'s brothers and sisters helped their parents with the farm. They didn't have much time for school. They spent long hot days in the sun picking cotton. Some chopped the cotton, and some took the seeds out of the fuzzy blossoms.

J.C.'s father wanted a better life for his family. In 1922 he sold his mule. The family used the money to move to Cleveland, Ohio.

Henry Owens could not find steady work in Cleveland. But J.C. could go to school. On his first day at his new school, the teacher asked J.C. what his name was. She heard him say "Jesse," not J.C. From then on, everyone called him Jesse.

Picking cotton was a hard way to make a living.

The Owens family moved to Cleveland, Ohio, in 1922. Like many other southern African Americans at this time, they moved north hoping for better jobs, education, and housing.

CHAPTER 2

The Buckeye Bullet

When Jesse was fourteen years old, the coach of the junior high school track team asked him to be on the team. The coach's name was Charles Riley. Every day Jesse got up early and met Coach Riley at the track.

Jesse's lungs were still bad, and he was often sick. He trained with Coach Riley every morning. Running helped Jesse's lungs, and he grew stronger. And he was even running faster.

By the time he was in high school, Jesse Owens was making a name for himself. Everybody at Cleveland East Technical High School was proud of his track records. He worked very hard to become a fast runner and a good jumper.

He ran dashes, and did high jumps and broad jumps (long jumps). And he broke national high school records almost every time he ran or jumped. Jesse was asked to come to Ohio State University and run for the track team. But he told track coach Larry Snyder that he could not go. Jesse had to work to help his family because his father still wasn't working.

When Jesse was in high school, he tied the world record for the 100-yard dash. He ran it in just 9.4 seconds.

Coach Snyder wanted Jesse to run on the Ohio State team. The coach

Ready, set, go! Jesse practiced a new starting position for running races.

Top: His old crouching style.

Bottom: With this new standing start, Jesse could get to full speed even faster.

At Ohio
State, Jesse
broke the
world broad
jump record
with a leap
of 26 feet
2 $\frac{1}{2}$ inches.

helped Henry Owens get a job as a janitor at the university. Now Jesse did not have to work to help his family. He could work to pay his own way through school.

Jesse trained harder and harder. He wanted to be the best. On May 25, 1935, Jesse broke three world records and tied another record at the University of Michigan at Ann Arbor.

The Ohio State sports teams were nicknamed the Buckeyes. So after that day, people started calling Jesse "the Buckeye Bullet." He was on his way to the 1936 Olympics in Berlin, Germany.

Jesse Owens, left, and Ralph Metcalfe competed in the Olympic track tryouts in 1936. Both athletes made the team.

CHAPTER 3

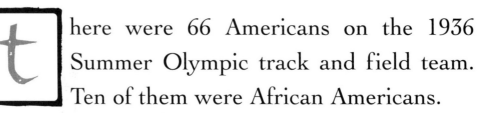

The Berlin Olympics

here were 66 Americans on the 1936 Summer Olympic track and field team. Ten of them were African Americans.

Adolf Hitler, the leader of Germany, came to the games on the opening day. The large crowd cheered for him. They raised their arms and shouted "Heil Hitler!"

Hitler was a Nazi. He believed that Germans were the "master race." He said they would rule the world one day. He also said that Jews and people of

**On his way to the 1936 Summer Olympics in Germany,
Jesse takes a practice jump aboard
the S.S. *Manhattan*.**

color were not equal to whites. Hitler hoped these Olympics would prove he was right.

Jesse Owens was the star of the 1936 Olympic Games. He won the 100-meter dash. Ralph Metcalfe, who was also an African American, came in second. Then, Jesse won the 200-meter dash. Matthew Robinson, another black man, came in second.

Other black athletes did very well too. Cornelius Johnson, David Albritton, and Delos Thurber won the gold, silver, and bronze medals in the high jump. Adolf Hitler was very upset.

This 1998 postage stamp honors Jesse's Olympic victory.

Jesse Owens, Six World Records

German leader Adolf Hitler wanted his athletes to win all the Olympic events. He was angry at the success of the African-American athletes.

"I was going to stay up in the air forever," said Jesse at the 1936 Olympics.

CHAPTER 4

A Good Sport

Jesse was doing very well at the Olympics. Then something went wrong in the broad jump event. People were surprised that the great Jesse Owens was in trouble. When he did his first jump, he thought it was a practice jump. But it wasn't. Now he had only two more tries. If he missed these jumps, he would not get into the final round.

Jesse got set. He did his next jump. "Scratched," the judge shouted. Jesse's foot was over the white line. The jump didn't count. He had

The U.S. Olympic track and field team stars. *Front row, from left:*
Cornelius Johnson, Jesse Owens, and Glenn Hardin.
Back row, from left: **Marty Glickman, Gene Venzke, Albert J.**
Mangin, Foy Draper, and Forrest G. Towns.

only one more jump left. If he missed this jump, he
was out.

Luz Long was a very good broad jumper. Luz
was Germany's best hope for a gold medal in this

event. He spoke to Jesse. His English was not very good. "I am Luz Long," he said. "You need to calm yourself." He smiled at Jesse. The two young men talked until Jesse felt calmer. Jesse's last jump was good. He would compete against Luz in the finals.

A gold medal with the Olympic torch.

Jesse beat Luz Long in the final broad jump and set a world record. Luz surprised everyone. He raised Jesse's arm and shouted, "Jesse . . . Jesse." The crowd joined in and shouted "Jesse . . . Jesse!" People cheered for both Jesse and Luz. They were both winners.

Jesse was also part of the 400-meter relay team. He was not part of the original team. Jesse and Ralph Metcalfe replaced the two starting American runners, named Marty Glickman and Sam Stoller.

Some people believe that Glickman and Stoller were replaced because they were Jewish. They were very angry. But Glickman and Stoller still cheered when the American 400-meter relay team won first place. Jesse had won another gold medal. He went home with four gold medals.

Jesse won his fourth gold medal as part of the 400-meter relay team. From left: Jesse Owens, Ralph Metcalfe, Foy Draper, and Frank Wykoff.

Jesse never saw Luz Long again. Luz was killed in World War II. After the war ended, Jesse went back to Germany. He visited Luz's family. Jesse told them what Luz had done for him at the Olympics. The families became friends.

Jesse Owens, standing on the podium, salutes during the Olympic medals ceremony. In front of him is Naoto Tajima of Japan. Behind him, his friend Luz Long of Germany gives the Nazi salute, with his arm outstretched.

CHAPTER 5

Reach for Greatness

esse had married his high school sweetheart, Ruth Solomon, in 1935. They had three daughters: Gloria, Beverly, and Marlene.

Jesse faced some tough times after the Olympics. When he first came home, Jesse was treated like a star. People offered him many business deals. Jesse tried to be fair and honest. He believed other people were fair and honest, too. He was wrong. A lot of people were not fair with Jesse. He lost a lot of money.

Jesse started some businesses that worked out well. Others failed. Jesse went back to Ohio State for a while. He was not a very good student.

Jesse enjoyed working with children. He was very good at working with kids and helping start athletic programs. He worked for the Recreation Department of Cook County (Chicago), Illinois. He told young children all over America to "reach for greatness."

This stamp was issued in 1990.

Many people worked for the rights of African Americans during the 1960s. African Americans did win some rights, but there was still prejudice. There were still many black people who were poor. They had little hope of doing better, and African Americans were angry.

"For a time at least, I was the most famous person in the entire world," said Jesse Owens. At this parade in New York City, fans cheered wildly as Jesse waved.

**1. Winning a broad jump event. 2. A track meet in college.
3. The Olympic champion. 4. Ruth Owens in 1996 with a statue
of her husband at the Jesse Owens Memorial Park
in Oakville, Alabama.**

Jesse wrote a book called *Blackthink* in 1970. He said that African Americans did not get ahead because they did not want to. Many people did not like the book. They wrote angry letters to Jesse. Some letters said that Jesse was too famous to know about the prejudice against many African Americans.

Jesse read the letters carefully. He thought again about the problems of African Americans. In 1972, he wrote another book, called *I Have Changed*. In this book, he apologized for some of the things he said in *Blackthink*.

Jesse Owens was given many honors in his life. In February 1979, President Jimmy Carter gave Jesse Owens an award at the White House. President Carter said, "He has always helped others to reach for greatness."

Jesse Owens died of lung cancer on March 31, 1980, in Tucson, Arizona. He was 66 years old.

timeLiNe

1913 — Born on September 12 in Oakville, Alabama.

1922 — Moves to Cleveland, Ohio.

1930 — Breaks national high school records in track.

1933 — Joins Ohio State University track team.

1935 — Breaks three world records in track and ties another one; marries Ruth Solomon.

1936 — Wins four gold medals at the Olympics in Berlin, Germany.

1937 –1950 — Works at many different jobs to support his wife and three daughters.

1950s — Helps start athletic programs for children.

1970 — Writes *The Jesse Owens Story* and *Blackthink: My Life as Black Man and White Man*.

1976 — Awarded the Presidential Medal of Freedom by President Gerald Ford.

1979 — Receives the Living Legend Award from President Jimmy Carter.

1980 — Dies on March 31.

936

936

1930

WORDS to KNOW

broad jump—A track and field event now called the long jump. Athletes compete to see how far they can jump. There are two events. In one, the athletes begin from a standing position. In the other, they get a running start.

bronze medal—The award that is given to the third place winner in Olympic events.

coach—A person who helps train and guide athletes in a specific sport.

dash—A short-distance running competition.

finals—The championship competition in a sporting event.

gold medal—The award that is given to the first place winner in Olympic events.

Heil Hitler—This German phrase means *Hail Hitler*—or *Praises to Hitler*.

high jump—A track and field event. Athletes compete to see who can jump the highest. The athletes jump over a high cross bar and try not to knock it off.

Hitler, Adolf—The Nazi leader of Germany from 1933 to 1945.

WORDS to KNOW

Nazi—The political party in power in Germany from 1933 to 1945.

Olympics—A sporting event where athletes from all over the world compete for medals in all kinds of sports. The first Olympics were held in ancient Greece. The new Olympics began in 1896. They are held every four years in different countries.

prejudice—A dislike of people, places, or things without a good reason.

president—The leader of a country or an organization.

silver medal—The award that is given to the second place winner in Olympic events.

track and field meet—A competition where the sports are running, jumping, and throwing.

world record—The best performance in the world of a sports event.

LeaRN moRe aBout Jesse Owens

Books

Adler, David A. *A Picture Book of Jesse Owens*. New York, N.Y.: Holiday House, Inc., 1992.

Hennessy, Barbara. *Olympics*. New York, N.Y.: Puffin Books, 2000.

Sutcliffe, Jane. *Jesse Owens*. Minneapolis, Minn.: Lerner Publishing Group, 2000.

Internet Addresses

Jesse Owens Museum

Click on Museum Tour for the Jesse Owens story, with lots of photos. Click on Articles for links to original news stories about Jesse.

<http://www.jesseowensmuseum.org/>

The Jesse Owens Foundation

This site has a biography and photographs of Jesse Owens.

<http://www.jesse-owens.org/about1.html>

index